SCOOBY-DOO!

A SCIENCE OF ENERGY MYSTERY

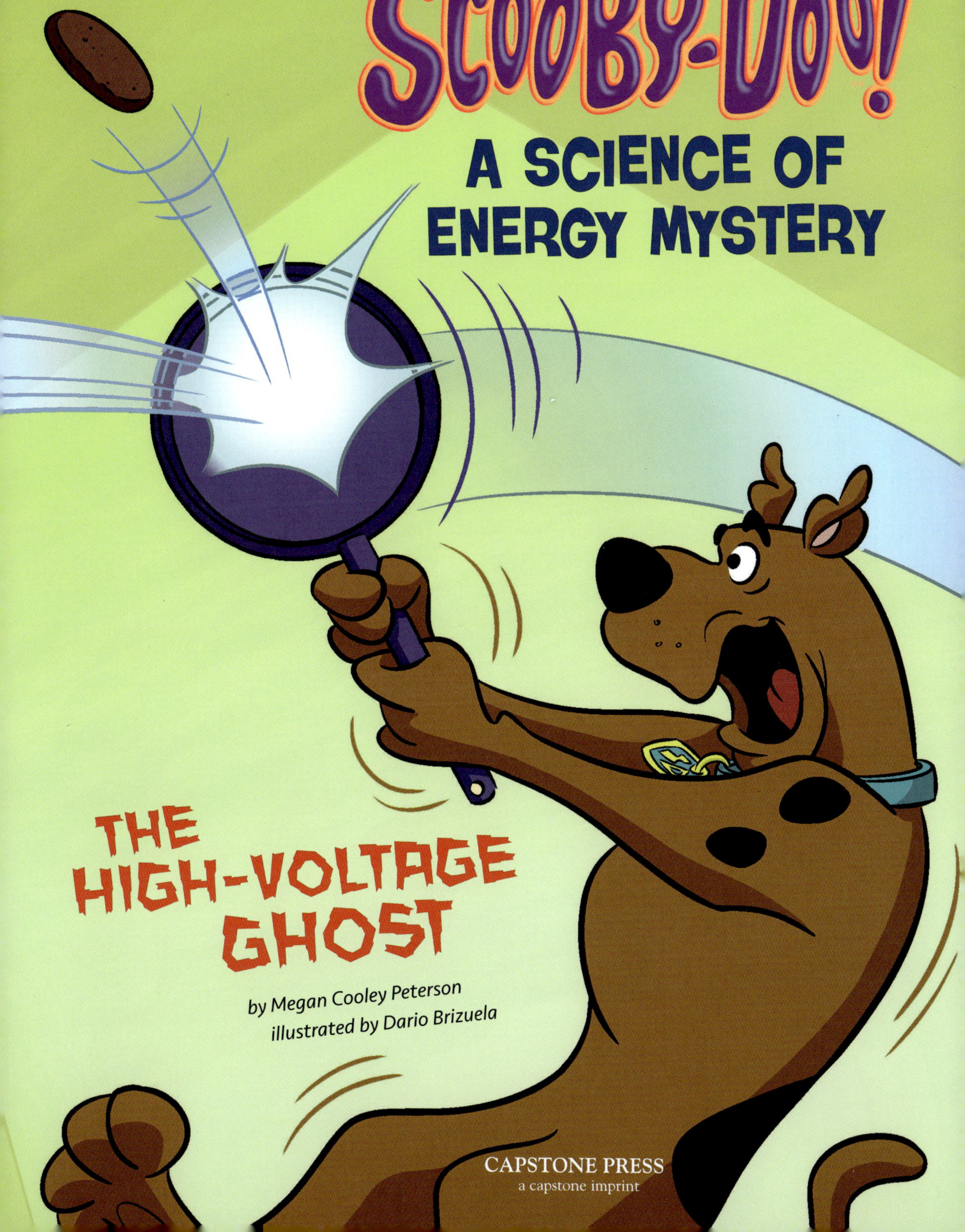

THE HIGH-VOLTAGE GHOST

by Megan Cooley Peterson
illustrated by Dario Brizuela

CAPSTONE PRESS
a capstone imprint

The gang drove the Mystery Machine up an icy mountain road.

"I can't wait to go skiing," Daphne said. "How close is your uncle's cabin?"

Fred gripped the steering wheel. "Not close enough," he said. "We're running out of gas!"

"And we're running out of heat," Shaggy said, shivering. "I can't feel my teeth!"

"It's way below zero," Daphne said.

"Ruh, roh," Scooby whimpered.

"There's a town a mile up the road," Velma said. "Maybe we can find some gas there."

"And something to eat," Shaggy added. "A plate of hamburgers would really warm me up."

"This place looks like a ghost town," said Daphne.

"It's probably not haunted," Velma said. "The electricity must just be out."

"Either way, the gas station is closed," Fred added. "And our tank is almost empty."

"Man, my stomach is as empty as our gas tank," Shaggy complained.

"Rine roo," said Scooby.

"I saw a ski lodge in town. Let's check it out," Daphne suggested.

"I'm Mayor Dudley," the man at the lodge said. "Welcome to Winterhaven."

"There hasn't been much of a welcome so far," Shaggy whined. "No hamburgers, no power, and only candles to keep us warm."

"The light and heat from candles are forms of energy," Velma said.

"Poor Scoob is trying to make his own heat," joked Shaggy.

"That's right," Daphne said. "Everything in the universe is made of atoms and molecules. When they move, they have heat energy. The faster the molecules move around, the warmer an object is."

"Rarm!" Scooby said, jumping up and down.

"Most towns use electricity for their energy. What happened to the electricity in Winterhaven, Mayor?" Fred asked.

"It's all because of the 10,000-Volt Ghost," the mayor said. "Let me tell you kids the story."

FACT FILE

Heat always flows from warmer objects to cooler objects. The molecules in a hot object bump into the molecules in a cold object. The cold object's molecules speed up and become warmer. That's why your hands get warmer when you hold a mug of hot chocolate.

Winterhaven was once a popular ski resort town. During a violent storm, trees blew over and knocked down power lines. The town lost power.
Mr. Collins, the power plant owner, sent a worker to fix the line. The worker climbed the power pole by himself.
Lightning hit the pole. The worker vanished as if into thin air.

"Zoinks!" cried Shaggy. "Lightning sure is spooky."

"It's not spooky, it's science. But it can be dangerous," Velma explained. "Lightning carries electrical energy."

"Where does electrical energy come from?" Shaggy asked.

"Electrons carry electrical energy," replied Fred. "An electron is a tiny particle inside an atom. The flow of electrons creates an electric current."

FACT FILE

Benjamin Franklin was an inventor and a scientist. He experimented with electricity in the 1700s. He also invented the lightning rod to keep people safe. Lightning strikes the tall, metal rod on top of a building instead of the building or people.

"The worker must have been struck by lightning," Daphne said. "Did anyone ever see him again?"

The mayor shivered. "I'm afraid not—but they saw his ghost," he said. "It returned to terrorize the town. It scared everyone away."

"Maybe we can help shed some light on this mystery," Fred offered. "Let's investigate the power plant."

"Like, how does a power plant work?" Shaggy asked.

"Power plants change the chemical energy stored in fossil fuels into electricity," Velma explained. "Coal and oil are kinds of fossil fuels."

"Power lines carry the electricity to homes, schools, and businesses," Fred added. "When you turn on a light bulb, the electricity becomes light energy."

"And a toaster changes electricity into heat energy," Daphne said.

Shaggy's stomach rumbled. "Man, I wish we had a toaster. I'm starving!"

"Rhost!" Scooby shouted.

"No time for toast now, Scoob," Fred said.

"Like, I think he meant *ghost!*" Shaggy exclaimed.

"Whew!" Shaggy said. "We thought you were the 10,000-Volt Ghost!"

"I'm Mr. Collins," the man said. "I own this power plant."

"Is the generator broken?" Velma asked.

Mr. Collins nodded. "Every time I get it fixed, it goes haywire. It must be the ghost."

"Why would a ghost care about a generator?" Velma wondered.

"I wish I knew," Mr. Collins said.

Daphne scooped sunflower seeds from the ground. "And how did these seeds get inside the plant?" she asked.

"It's a clue! Let's split up, gang," Fred said. "Shaggy, Scooby, and Velma can check out the cafeteria here in the plant. Daphne and I will head to the pet shop in town to see if they're missing birdseed."

"We'll meet you later at the pet shop!" said Velma.

"Man, these frozen hamburger patties really bum me out," Shaggy said. "If we had some electricity, I could cook us up a feast!"

Scooby licked his lips. "Rum!" he said.

"Quick, Scoob! Think fast," Shaggy said, winding up.

"Shaggy, did you know your arm holds potential energy?" Velma asked.

"So, like, what happens when I throw this meat-sicle?" Shaggy asked.

"The stored energy in your arm moves into the hamburger and becomes kinetic energy. Energy transfers happen all the time," Velma said.

"Did you hear that, Scoob?" Shaggy asked. "You, like, totally rang that hamburger's bell!"

"The sound of the frying pan hitting the frozen burger is also a form of energy," Velma said.

"Renergy?" Scooby asked.

"Yes, Scooby. When atoms and molecules in the air vibrate, they make a sound. Sound energy travels through the air in waves," Velma said.

"Zoinks! The meat-sicle hit the ghost!" Shaggy shouted.

"And it doesn't look very happy," Velma said. "Let's get out of here!"

FACT FILE

Sound energy is invisible, but you can feel it. Hold an empty plastic bottle against a speaker. Turn up the volume. You can feel the sound moving through the bottle!

"Those seeds definitely came from this pet shop," Daphne said.

"And they lead into that room," Fred said.

Velma pointed to the couch. "It looks like someone, or something, is living here."

"Scoob, don't eat all the evidence," said Shaggy. "It might be an important clue."

Fred walked toward the door. "Only one way to find out."

"Here we go again," Shaggy muttered.

"This snowsuit's cold and damp—someone just used it," Velma said. "Something strange is going on in this town."

"Look!" Fred exclaimed. "Scooby found a secret hatch!"

"Let's see where it leads," Daphne said.

"It's a long secret tunnel," Fred said. "I wonder where it goes."

Shaggy yawned. "Man, all this walking is making me sleepy."

"I'm not surprised. Everything that moves uses energy," Velma said. "We can trace the energy we're using now back to the sun."

"The sun sure would be helpful right about now!" Shaggy said, holding up a flashlight.

"Light energy comes from the sun. Plants absorb the light," Velma continued.

"Then plants change the light into chemical energy," added Daphne. "The process is called photosynthesis."

"Like, I'm not a plant," Shaggy said, chomping on the seeds.
"But you're eating one," Velma said. "Every time you eat, you are part of an energy chain."
"All energy flows through an energy chain," Daphne explained. "Our bodies take in chemical energy from the food we eat. This energy is stored as fat and other substances."
"When you move, your muscles turn the stored energy into kinetic energy," Fred said.
ROOK!

"Just as I suspected," Velma said. "This tunnel leads right to the power plant."

"Let's check out the power plant worker's house. Maybe we'll find another clue there," said Fred.

"This place is a mess," Shaggy said. "It's, like, even messier than my bedroom!"

"Winterhaven might still be running if it used other forms of energy," said Velma.

"Like what?" asked Shaggy.

"My family uses solar power to generate electricity," Velma explained. "Solar panels change the sun's light energy into electricity."

"Solar energy is also better for the environment," Daphne added. "Burning fossil fuels at the power plant causes pollution."

"I found something, gang," said Fred. "This letter lists pieces of land in Winterhaven. It was sent to the power plant worker."

"Let's go to the courthouse and follow up on this clue," Velma suggested.

"Hey, Scooby," Shaggy said. "Why was the math book so sad?"

"I ron't row," answered Scooby.

"Because it had so many problems!" said Shaggy.

"Enough with the silly jokes," Velma said. "I found something! This records book says Mayor Dudley bought the land listed in the letter."

"But what does it all mean?" Daphne asked.

"I'm not quite sure yet, but I'll bet that ghost has some answers," Velma said.

"Let's use science to trap this ghost," Daphne said. "We'll raise the net with the rope to give the net potential energy."

Fred tightened the rope. "We'll wait for the ghost to show up and then let the net drop. When the net falls, its potential energy will become kinetic energy."

"Who knew science could come in so handy?" asked Shaggy.

"Now it's time to see who this ghost really is," Daphne said, peeling off the ghost's mask.

"Just as I suspected," Velma said. "It's the power plant worker! He's the one who kept breaking the generator."

"How'd you guess?" Daphne asked.

"Let's find the sheriff," Velma said. "I'll explain everything then."

"Clever disguise," added Fred. "The worker rigged up a snowsuit using batteries. A battery holds chemical energy, which is turned into electricity. The batteries lit up his glowing suit. Not a 10,000-Volt Ghost after all."

"What is the meaning of this?" Mayor Dudley asked.

"The records show you bought a bunch of land in Winterhaven—after the ghost scared everyone away," Velma explained.

"You got the land dirt cheap," added Fred.

"It looks like you planned to sell it for a huge profit after the ghost story died down," Daphne said. "You and your worker made up the whole thing."

"And we would've gotten away with it if it hadn't been for you meddling kids!" said the mayor.

"Now that we have that settled, let's get the power back on and go fry up those meat-sicles," Shaggy said. "I'm starving!"

"Re roo!" said Scooby.

GLOSSARY

atom (AT-uhm)—the smallest particle of an element

chemical energy (KE-muh-kuhl EN-uhr-jee)—the energy of a substance that is released through a chemical reaction

electricity (i-lek-TRIS-i-tee)—the movement of electrons that can be used to make light and heat or to make machines work

electron (i-LEK-tron)—a tiny particle in an atom that travels around the nucleus

energy (EN-uhr-jee)—the ability to do work, such as moving things or giving heat or light

fossil fuels (FAH-suhl FYOOLZ)—natural fuels formed from the remains of plants and animals; coal, oil, and natural gas are fossil fuels

generator (JEN-uh-ray-tur)—a machine that produces electricity by turning a magnet inside a coil of wire

kinetic energy (ki-NET-ik EN-uhr-jee)—the energy of a moving object

molecule (MOL-uh-kyool)—the atoms making up the smallest unit of a substance; H_2O is a molecule of water

photosynthesis (foh-toh-SIN-thuh-siss)—the process by which green plants make their food

potential energy (puh-TEN-shuhl EN-uhr-jee)—energy stored within an object, waiting to be released

solar power (SOH-luhr POW-uhr)—energy from the sun that can be used for heating and electricity.

vibrate (VYE-brate)—to move back and forth quickly

SCIENCE AND ENGINEERING PRACTICES

1. Asking questions (for science) and defining problems (for engineering)

2. Developing and using models

3. Planning and carrying out investigations

4. Analyzing and interpreting data

5. Using mathematics and computational thinking

6. Constructing explanations (for science) and designing solutions (for engineering)

7. Engaging in argument from evidence

8. Obtaining, evaluating, and communicating information

Next Generation Science Standards

READ MORE

Biskup, Agnieszka. *Aliens and Energy.* Monster Science. Mankato, Minn.: Capstone Press, 2012.

Bow, James. *Energy from the Sun: Solar Power.* Next Generation Energy. New York: Crabtree Publishing, 2016.

Maloof, Torrey. *Transferring Energy.* Huntington Beach, Calif.: Teacher Created Materials, 2016.

INTERNET SITES

FactHound offers a safe, fun way to find Internet sites related to this book. All of the sites on FactHound have been researched by our staff.

Here's all you do:

Visit *www.facthound.com*

Type in this code: 9781515725916

INDEX

Thanks to our adviser for his expertise, research, and advice:
Paul Ohmann, PhD, Associate Professor of Physics
University of St. Thomas, St. Paul, Minnesota

Published in 2016 by Capstone Press, A Capstone Imprint
1710 Roe Crest Drive, North Mankato, Minnesota 56003
www.mycapstone.com

Library of Congress Cataloging-in-Publication Data
Names: Peterson, Megan Cooley, author.
Title: Scooby-Doo! a science of energy mystery : the high-voltage ghost / by Megan Cooley Peterson.
Other titles: Science of energy mystery
Description: North Mankato, Minnesota : Capstone Press, a Capstone imprint,
[2016] | 2016 | Series: Scooby-Doo! Scooby-Doo solves it with S.T.E.M. |
Includes bibliographical references and index. | Audience: ages 9-12. | Audience: grades 4 to 6.
Identifiers: LCCN 2015043264 | ISBN 9781515725916 (library binding) | ISBN 9781515726524 (ebook
PDF) Subjects: LCSH: Force and energy—Juvenile literature. | Scooby-Doo
(Fictitious character)—Juvenile literature.
Classification: LCC QC73.4 .P46 2016 | DDC 531/.6—dc23
LC record available at http://lccn.loc.gov/2015043264

Editorial Credits
Editor: Kristen Mohn
Designer: Ashlee Suker
Creative Director: Nathan Gassman
Production Specialist: Gene Bentdahl
The illustrations in this book were created digitally.

Printed in the United States of America.
032016 009681F16

OTHER TITLES IN THIS SET:

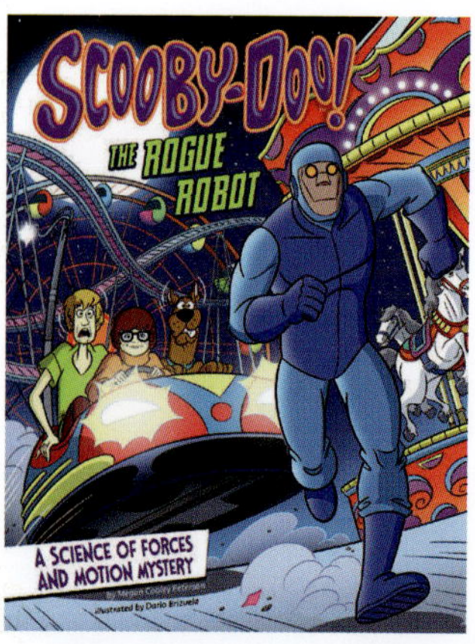